T0146612

VETERAN
VIA
GRACE

VETERAN
VIA
GRACE
ONE LIFE WITH GOD IN COMMAND

JAMES MARTIN FEEZEL

 iUniverse®

VETERAN VIA GRACE
ONE LIFE WITH GOD IN COMMAND

iUniverse books may be ordered through booksellers or by contacting:

iUniverse
1663 Liberty Drive
Bloomington, IN 47403
www.iuniverse.com
1-800-Authors (1-800-288-4677)

ISBN: 978-1-5320-3760-3 (sc)
ISBN: 978-1-5320-3761-0 (e)

Library of Congress Control Number: 2017917879

Print information available on the last page.

iUniverse rev. date: 11/20/2017

Chapter One

THE EARLY YEARS

I T WAS AUGUST 15, 1925 in the small town of Wood River, Illinois that a baby boy was born to James and Helen Feezel. This would be the third child but first son of this young family. However, the grandfather, Helen's father was not impressed. His statement was, as later told me, "young man you are cutting off Toody's nose." Toody in this instance was slightly older sister Helen Louise Feezel who had arrived in the household May 28, 1924. George Martin Eyestone was however, a loved and respected visitor at this moment living with his 6th child, his youngest daughter and family. The head of the household and my father was James Millison Feezel, 27-year-old Naval veteran of WW1 having relocated quite recently from his home on a farm in Fayette County, IL. The relocation was facilitated by procurement of a job with the new oil refinery Standard Oil Company of Indiana. Standard had established this location in 1906, ultimately joined by a Shell Oil refinery and an independent known as Wood River Oil. Oil refining began producing heating oil, kerosene and coke even before there was a city, which formed in 1909. Standard purchased two dozen homes from Sears Roebuck Co. to provide worker housing. However, by 1928 and less than 10 short years of Dad's time at Standard, the promising economy in our great developing country was losing the shine; depression seemed to be taking hold. Now my father and mother for that matter had lived on farms and knew about living off the ground. Dad worried he might lose his job, but "at least I'll feed my family," he said. Thus, a small farm was sought, and we moved to a very rural home in the area south of Roxana/Wanda. Of course, I knew little of this at that time, but it did seem to occur exactly on my third birthday. I do believe there had been some celebrating and I had supposed this was just a visit. So, I sidled up to mom who was cranking the Victrola for another record and I asked, "Mommy, after you play that record can we go home?" She replied, "Darling, we are home, and I think I shall see you to bed."

Farm Home 1935

This may have interest only to me, but I recall this as my first conscious memory and recall it clearly yet today. Then followed years of gardens, pigs, chickens, turkeys, even a milk cow, not to mention the wild dewberries and raspberries. Yes, we had a few close calls with snakes. Of course, who of my age doesn't remember that long cold walk from the back door to that lovely two-hole outhouse in the far backyard. Then you hurry back in to a love affair with that big old potbellied stove in the kitchen.

Now let's take a brief pause for Genealogy. Typically, we as children fail to give proper thought and respect for our parents and those before us. Through the years (largely thanks to research by my brother Jerry David Feezel, who was a late arrival to the family in 1938), I have learned that my family name is traceable six generations back to Phillip Martin Feezel, my 4th great-grandfather. He was born in 1716 in Essenheim, Germany. Phillip sailed for America in 1738, lived in Pennsylvania, and later in Virginia, passing on May 28, 1789 in Bedford, VA.

In the generations down to me there were many ladies with last names such as Limbaugh, Foulks, Huffman, McGowan, Engler, and my mom, Helen Eyestone. Her family we have also traced to a German origin in the Black Forest region, the small town Ellmendingen. The first Eyestone to immigrate to the U.S. was George Martin Augenstein, who left Germany in 1830 with his family. George Sr. died at sea of Cholera in 1832. However, George Martin Jr. (2nd great-grandfather) proceeded and took up residence initially in Pennsylvania and then Ohio. Eventually the family settled on farm lands of East Central Illinois in Fayette County. There my parents joined in matrimony when that good-looking sailor came home from the war in 1919. As you may note, my middle name was present in both sides of my German heritage. This genealogical fact I take with much pride.

Now back to the farm, and in a few short years it is off to school in that small town of Wanda.

Wanda School class 1932

When I say small town, I mean fewer than 20 houses. So, at school the first thing I had to learn was that outside, the big boys ruled. As an outsider (living three miles away) I had to fight the local first grader. This was a messy affair fortunately broken up by the Principal/senior teacher. That other fighter was Donnie Woods who became a good friend, but more about him later.

Thus, I spent my next five years in this two-room school where each vertical row of desks represented one school grade. Yes, I did progress normally from row to row. The building had a full basement where were located restrooms, a coat room, and an area to eat our lunches or spend recess time on inclement days. It also served as a storm shelter when weather threatened. Just across a large looping driveway stood the local Methodist Church. Still a place of worship today, the current brick building was erected in 1935. However, the earlier site had served religious services since 1802. Prior to that time a log cabin had stood on site for protection from raiding Indians.

The lands in this general area were very sandy soil, ideal for growing watermelon and cantaloupe. I did love those melons and there was always a large patch to be raided if you were desperate. However, about a country mile up the road a widowed lady managed at least part of her living selling melons from her front yard. My sister Louise and I would often stop on our way home from school. This grand lady enjoyed our visits so much she was always willing to open a ripe melon for the occasion. This three-mile trip to and from school was very often done on foot but later via bicycle.

Transportation in these years was young and rapidly developing. I recall Dad's first family auto had no glass beyond the windshield. Side curtains, as they were called, consisted of fabric bordering a window of isinglass. Yet by the time I was about 10 our family car did have hand-cranked glass side windows. It was in this auto one Sunday we started to church, Dad at the wheel and we three in back. Oh my, the car stalled just on top of the railroad tracks, and sure enough, here came a train. I believe Dad might have frozen in fear and I was thinking how do I abandon this metal can. Mom rushed out the door, in front of the car, telling Dad to get it out of gear. Then she pushed that car back off the train tracks. Mothers—never underestimate them!

Modernizing the Farm

A next phase of my education came as handyman for my dad as the Rural Electrification program came to our area in 1935. I had most likely gained some familiarity with the grand attic area of this old farmhouse. It was partially floored with a couple of gabled areas and windows where one could gaze out over much of the farm lands. Adding electricity justified getting my hands on, stringing the very earliest version of Romex wiring to the center of each room as well as down walls for outlets and switches. This was actually a newer version of wiring compared with that which existed in the homes of Wood River; it consisted of two single strands of wire cradled in ceramic insulators. With this ability to retire the candle and kerosene lamps, it didn't take Dad long to think in terms of upgrading plumbing and heating systems. First Dad found enough space in the Fruit cellar to place the electric pump and pressurized tank very near the well that had supplied the hand pump at the kitchen sink. Space for the oil-fired furnace, however, would require more under floor space Than the old fruit cellar. So, we proceeded to remove a section of the back-wall foundation. (Pop must have had some structural engineering ability.) From there we began to excavate firm earth. Dad soon taught me the process of water boring with a hose supplied to a length of small diameter pipe. At any rate, I was soon carving out great cubes of earth in approx. three-foot chunks and managing to fall them on a wooden skid we had generated for the program. We did not own a tractor and I certainly could not pull that skid, but by then dad had allowed me enough time with the truck in the pasture to master the clutch.

I well remember my first shot at this function. We were in the garden with a load of fertilizer. Pop said, "OK jump in crank it up and pull forward a few feet." Well I had watched lots, so I proceeded with the mechanics. However, as I tried to let that left foot come up with the clutch the little truck began to act a bit like an untamed horse. Pop said, "throw out the clutch." My interpretation was to take my foot off that sucker. No, <u>bad move!</u> That last "buck" almost dumped the load on him.

But this excavation project was at least a year later, and I could use the truck to pull that heavy skid load up an incline and into the location pop had designated for our earthen pile. In time, mostly mine, enough space had been generated to provide what was needed to install a newfangled oil burning furnace. Thereafter we had warm air piped to each room of the house in the winter. Summer was another deal, and the only air-conditioning we knew was move the air or get where it was moving. Also, you'd wear as little clothing as you could get away with.

Somewhere in this modernization period, Dad brought home an electric motor for Mom's Briggs & Stratton gas-powered washing machine. I proceeded to make the conversion to electric. I need to note that we were in a period of rapid technology growth. I personally recall Mom's clothes washing progressing from scrub-board to a mechanized machine where the tub contained an agitator hung from the lid and rotated by a wooden rack & pinion system. The "motor" power was one feller tall enough and stout enough to push that hinged tiller back and forth. Washing next progressed to the more favorably functioning gas engine, which I removed for the electric motor.

Well it wasn't long till I looked at my bicycle, then at that now spare gas engine and concluded I need to marry up those two. So, with various materials salvaged such as a roller from an old washer wringer, pullies, and a belt purchased by Dad, I had a motor bike.

Motor Bike & Gramps

Thus in 1939-40 high school was some seven miles from home (back in Wood River). Since I had no car nor legal status to drive one, I often used my new motorbike for transport. One afternoon coming home, fate allowed me to encounter a neighboring farm friend headed home on a small Farmall tractor. My vehicle had no speedometer but his did. Naturally I prevailed on him for a speed check. Our meeting had occurred at straight and open highway with very little traffic. After about a mile run, where we turned off the highway, Mr. Hessle reported we had been running right at 30 mph. Not bad I thought for a home-built bike.

Motor Bike & House

Back home, upgrade work was not yet finished because the next dream was to eliminate that most unloved outhouse. Technology was at hand; we had a pressured water system, but just needed the indoor space, equipment and plumbing. It also required an outside buried receiving tank. Since Dad was still boss and I the apprentice, you know who drew the outside assignment. Besides I had proven earth moving skills. Eventually we had this warm indoor restroom and bathing facility. In the process, I had learned how to fit water pipe, lead a joint in cast iron drain pipe, and some carpentry also.

Little did I realize that I was only a few years away from a forced need to relearn how to exist in very rough circumstances. But it may also have been quite providential that just a few years or months earlier I had a significant and profound moment in my religious education. You may recall the mention of the historic Wanda church. I had been no stranger to this institution but a regular, emphasized by both parents, but especially by Mom. During one of the occasions of travel to a Christian youth meeting, I had experienced a sudden awareness of my "lack of couth." At the closing ceremony, I dropped to my knee and with a private call to God I confessed my need for "a remake." I asked him to take charge of my life and I would do my very best to become such a man as He might have pride in. I am certain of a special moment with sudden awareness of a dear lady standing quietly at my side (Aunt Nettie to my sis and I). Change, if any was expected or noted, was subtle and not dwelled upon.

As noted I had spent my first five school years at Wanda, but for purposes I faintly recall we were residing in Wood River (WR) for my 6th grade year. This must have been my one year of art discovery and I well remember the teacher allowing or assigning me to create an Easter border atop three walls of the school-room. So with colored chalks I created Easter bunnies and eggs in an eight-inch border. I also well recall the area of our house, its proximity to the home of my Aunt Minnie and Uncle Les Harrod as well as to his auto garage. I had one particular friend just across the street named Melvin Engleman. There was also next door a female friend and it may have been about then I began to take some note of the differences. However, next and the remainder of my school years were back at the much-improved farm home. With some thought and research, I realized this temporary residence had allowed my mother to be nearer to medical help while preparing for the birth of my brother, Jerry David Feezel.

By this time my oldest sis, Cleta, as a flowering late teenager was causing the young men to find the home. One of the most frequent of those was a young man named Gordon Roseberry who came riding in on a beautiful palomino pony. Ultimately, years later they did ride off together into matrimony. However, this was only shortly before the turmoils of the world seriously altered our lives.

Conflict Abroad

The onset of this change was thrust upon my consciousness on the evening of December 7, 1941. I well remember I was at the WR Bowling Alley, for I was employed in evenings and week-ends as a pin-setter. Pin setting in those days was not mechanized. It was one lad who leapt into the pit, hoisted the ball to the elevated return track, placed the pins in a spotting rack, and pulled it down to position the standing pins. The fun and chatter of this evening was suddenly shattered by the radio announcement that we had been attacked by Japan.

At this point in the march of time I was a junior in High school. Changes seemed to be noticeable everywhere and even I became more attentive to news and political-military events. My dad seemed to be much more occupied at the plant, with the loading of a steady stream of tanker trucks. At the light oils terminal where he was a Foreman they were daily loading products such as Kerosene, Aviation fuel, three grades of auto fuel, and heating oils. Military recruiting stations sprang up and a draft program was initiated. By 1940, even before the Pearl Harbor event, a Military Conscription Program had become law, as upwards of 70% of the population believed our military intervention would become necessary. I was not to reach the registration age until 1943. However, numerous fellow students began to cut short their final school year to get an early start in their preferred service. Aware of this, however, my father spoke thus with me. "Jim, this war is going to involve you soon enough; please just wait and let it happen." Thus with considerable respect for the hearts of my parents, I finished school in May 1943 still not 18. Though I certainly did not finish as valedictorian, I had not flunked anything and only once had to negotiate with a teacher to get passed.

With a fresh Diploma in hand and probably the summer available (for work, no travel) I sought major employment. I was hired at the local steel mill, Laclede Steel. There I was led to a coil slitting machine, trained to both set-up and operate, and a week later my trainer said, "You got it; you know where the tool shop is, keep your tools sharp and stay careful." Mid-August I registered with Uncle, and by September I had that famous "Invitation by Friends and Neighbors." Maybe they were anxious to have me out of town! With Laclede Steel it was not so. The boss just said, "hand me that piece of paper & I will take care of it." I said, "Thank you sir, but no, I want to go do my part." I suppose at 18 we are a lot of "Dumb," but I had ultimate visions of myself beyond the steel mill. At least those "friends and neighbors" sent me in style to the Chicago Induction Center.

Chapter Two

THE WAR YEARS

I RODE THE ABE LINCOLN LUXURY fast train to Chicago. This involved some major part of October and I, like so very many young men of that day, desired to be assigned to the Air Force service for pilot training. I must have had something going for me [or was someone upstairs voting] at the eye exam station as I quickly knew I was not doing well; but the exam team kept with me almost coaching me, but in the end had to say, "Sorry son, your degree of color rendition is just outside the box and that could be dangerous." My heart was not into Navy but something of Dad's history caused me to ask. I was almost pleased when they said, "No their rule is the same, but the Army will be glad to have you." So, I was sent back home with an Army uniform, a two week leave and paper saying, "Report to Fort Knox, KY" sometime in November.

Soldier with Family,1943

Dad and my sister Cleta escorted me to Fort Knox and we had a pleasant tour of the camp and the Museum of the WWI armaments. Little recorded history and less memory provide early details, but it seems we merely spent several weeks at bunkhouse training and calisthenics and then Christmas leave. About January 2nd serious training began, five- mile hikes, many with "old agony hill" involved. Learning disassembling and reassembling personal firearms was next. Finally, target practice with the several small arms was added. Then we had to learn how to crawl while a 30 cal. machine gun laces the air just above you. Eventually we began to learn all the details of the several armored vehicles—the M5 Stuart or Light Tank, then the M4 Sherman Medium Tank, and the M3 Halftrack. With time I learned to drive all of them, and the Halftrack may have been the most dangerous. If you had failed to adhere to the instructor's advice, you would soon learn never to put your thumbs inside the steering wheel. Learning to drive the tanks was more fun as was learning to sight and fire the big gun. However, the Army liked to profess those monsters had a stabilizing system to allow firing on the run, and I enjoyed my chance to try. I seriously doubt there was ever much firing on the run in actual need, at least not where terrain such as that at training existed. Soon I learned in real action, "stop, fire, then move."

Footnote to younger readers--compared with today, yes, it sounds primitive. Please be aware that reference to my experience and equipment is from 70+ years ago. I am not unaware of our progress. I have personally seen and yes been in one of our fantastic Abram tanks. I have also had the pleasure of sitting with and hearing from General Montgomery Meigs III, the son of our battalion commander killed in France, after his experiences with a command of these tanks (2nd Armored Division in Desert Storm). They not only could stay on target, they could destroy one beyond their optical vision range.

Back to Knox 1944, there was a schedule and ultimately we had reached the end of that basic period. Thank God for the end of those five-mile walks, strenuous exercise and exhaustion, but I had to concede there was no fat on me and my 140 lb. frame now was 160 lb. It had caused me to want that "chow" regardless of quality.

Now we were to experience another close physical exam. I do not believe we were told the purpose was to test for adequate readiness for combat, but so be it. In my case it seemed a mysterious hand said not now. As the young doctor was sounding my chest there was a clicking sound with each breath. It was so audible one did not need a stethoscope. The good man merely said I do not know what this is, but you need to hang around for more observation. There were others and perhaps some just chosen for vehicle service.

With this reprieve from immediate transport to conflict we were reassembled and told that for the next three months we would spend time in both classroom training and hands-on activity. Our schedule would be more typical of a work week and we would be allowed frequent week-end off campus passes. We were also told that we could now have the privilege of an on-camp vehicle if we so desired. This last information was quickly passed to my father's ears with considerable anticipation on my part and I realized later probably considerable stress to him. We were still on the farm and Dad had a wonderful 1940 Ford sedan and a pickup truck. The pickup I was not so interested in, but I do believe it was newer than the model A version which I had two years earlier driven to Champagne-Urbana loaded with buddies for the State Basketball Tournament. That was a costly trip for it seemed we bought almost as much oil as we did gasoline.

However, back to the point, I pressed Dad to let me take the sedan back to camp. With my new maturity, and his yet fresh memory of WW1, can you picture with me his stress? Surely his mind was thinking, here is my 18-year-old son being trained for ground combat in another terrible conflict in Europe. Can I deny him this opportunity for some moments of good life?

Well he did not, and I drove the '40 Ford back to Fort Knox. I very shortly came to know a dear lady hostess at the Louisville USO. That lady was Mrs. Sherman (Nancy) Lodewick who promised to always have dates available for me and my buddies.

Nancy Lodewick, 1944

Soon, my "three musketeers" and I were accepting her offer. The musketeers were Jimmy Coon, Jack Kearny and George Walsch. Soon the young ladies were regulars also--by name Jane Barns, Libby Bazzel, Connie Bittenback, and George's girl I forgot. We toured sights such as Mammoth Cave and had parties in the Lodewick's backyard.

Party, Lodewick Yard

We were putting some miles on the Ford and the extra gasoline stamps Mr. Lodewick, as a banker, managed for us was also appreciated. However, time flies when you are having fun and soon it was new assignments for all. Me, to Camp Chaffee, Arkansas, where I had some extended field training. The most memorable was the 50 cal. targeting the flyovers. We were to shoot the balloons trailing the planes not the planes. I always wondered how they got the pilots to volunteer. Well I didn't kill any and had a perfect record of allowing no balloon to pass me. You would think I should have become a gunner somewhere, but this was the Army. By the end of summer a fresh inspection found me fit and off by train to the port of New York. It was Fall, and I most probably had been given leave time home with family, including a quick trip to Louisville and a last goodbye with my lady Jane. There, she added a St. Christopher medal to my Dog Tag identification chain.

Lady Jane, 1944

Shipping Out

Thus, late October I arrived at the port of NY, where with young soldiers by the thousands I marched up the gang plank aboard a ship of a mammoth size I had never seen before. It must have had a name but that never registered in my memory. Ultimately, we pulled away from the dock and out into the Bay, but there we waited, for what I wondered, three days at least had passed. Finally, we were under way again.

Now the shores of comforting lands were disappearing, but low to my left and to my right there were more ships, big ones and small ones and some with huge guns on deck. As we steamed on into the Great Atlantic Ocean it seemed the Armada grew until as far as I could see it seemed there were ships. Then one day the explanation came, for out on the south rim of the fleet, it appeared one of our battleships was rolling huge drums over the side and shortly a muffled thud of underwater explosion. This scenario continued for a short while and we sailed on.

I never seemed to care for the claustrophobic quarters or the sway of the hammock below deck, so I spent much time on deck with a couple of friends. One day the sea became quite troubled and the waves were so large as to be breaking over the front of the ship. So we thought, hey the real coaster ride is up there. We went to the bow peered over the rail to watch the water slide down as we lifted 50 or more feet above. Then watched again as the ocean rushed up the point of the ship till at the last minute we ducked under the rail as water flew over our heads. Really how fortunate we were to be here rather than sick below deck. Even taking a little food when you felt up to doing so was a challenge. You stood at a high table with a ledge all around to keep it all from sliding to the floor as the ship rolled. It took 11 days to cross the Atlantic with not a great deal to pass the time. There were plenty of "crap" poker games. The best education I had here was "stay out of them."

As we neared England the convoy was as you might say disassembling. The channel was too busy for us, so we sailed north and around Ireland and Scotland to land at Liverpool. There we clambered off again with all we owned in that duffel bag and boarded a train south to Southampton.

It seemed I had barely gotten my land legs back, maybe at best one meal under belt, and we were hustled onto a small ship, actually an LCT (landing craft, tank) to be beached at Normandy. Please note, this was not the initial invasion; landings had begun almost five months earlier and the actual exchange of fire had moved inland by various accounts. By beaching, I mean quite literally. This craft was flat bottomed with the very front hinged to drop for a loading and unloading platform. So, in the midst of a rainstorm and still in two feet of water, off we went onto muddy beach, facing at least 80 feet of Cliff. That I managed to haul my carcass and that heavy duffel up that slimy cliff is a testament to army training in the1940's.

Next, we were ordered to crack out our pup tents and in buddy system, one on best ground you could find, one pitched over, crawl in for the night. [Pup tents were the usually one man canvas sided weather shelter.] The Army pup tent would accommodate two bodies side by side and with one on the ground, hopefully separating you from the mud.

Starting the Ventures

So here am I about the 5th day of November 194 4 in France, shivering cold and wet as a drowned rat but thanking God that no one is shooting at me. I cannot help but remember a story circulated which I don't swear to any validity. Reportedly in the late 1900's a veteran flew into France and was challenged for his entry permit. His answer, "Hell, the last time I came into France no one was asking me for permission." Thus, it was a "test of your immune system night" and I didn't fare too well. At least the next day a good old Army 2½ ton truck picked us up to start inland. That night or perhaps next we were offered hospitality for the night under roof by a gracious and thankful French gentleman.

As he observed me rolling out my bedroll he appreciated the bad state of my head cold. He promptly advised, "Soldier with your permission I will treat your illness; give me your mess kit." I believe I would have accepted any offer of help. So with that he poured a liberal supply of what he identified as potato snoops in the one side, lit it with match and let it flame almost to boiling. He snuffed the flame with the top half of the kit, handed it to me and said, "drink it down." I let it cool just to not burn my lips and complied. That warm liquid went down **_good_**! I believe within five minutes I was horizontal and asleep. Probably eight hours later I awoke feeling so good I believe I could've tackled a full squad of Germans.

For the next two weeks, we traveled and subsisted on dry K rations and occasionally poorly warmed C-rations. Then, like it was thanksgiving, a chow wagon caught up to us and we had a supposedly kitchen prepared meal. I have to believe they would have failed the "Kitchen Corps" test, for within 24 hours everyone on board that truck was violently ill. Well we luckily found a small stream with a low concrete wall. What a sight that must have been; for there we were strung along that wall like pigeons with fortunately someone walking down the line handing out rolls of toilet paper.

I learned later we were not behind schedule because the original division was also making its way to their target area to relieve the very tired 4th Armored Div. of Patton's Third Army who had been severely damaged by the German 11th Panzer Div. near the town Rohrbach. By December 8th the 12th Armored Div. was on the front line—facing the enemy's 11th Panzer and live fire. On this first day there were some gains but also losses of both tanks and men. December 9th and 10th are well described in "History of the 23rd Tank Battalion." On December 11th, Col. Montgomery C. Meigs, commanding the 23rd Tank Battalion, was maneuvering his troops to continue the thrust against a well-positioned and concealed enemy. Col. Meigs had positioned his own tank so he could observe for gunfire and having just observed such had ordered his driver to back up. However, this hardly had left his lips when an 88 round crashed through his open hatch and he was killed instantly.

Assigned to a Tank

The morning report of December 12, 1944 shows three persons reporting to Headquarters of the 23rd Tank Battalion--Col. William A. Edwards, Major Jerome L. Schrader, and Pvt. James M. Feezel. I was shortly introduced to the other crew of Capt. William L. Comfort's tank to which I had just been assigned as Assistant Driver/Bow Gunner.

Tank with 3 crew, Dec.'44
Author @ lower left

This tank carried the identity S-3 as Capt. Comfort was Operations Officer. My position carried the rank of T-5 which I shortly acquired. The tank driver was T-4 Arthur Ostergaard. There was one other tank in this group known as the HQ. Co. Tank Section and I was introduced to at least some of them. I believe I will never forget T-4 Alvin Wolke who was busy cleaning the bloody area of the Gunner's position which he held in the battalion commanders tank. The next several days were quiet for the 23rd Tank Btn. as other elements of the 12th continued to take control of the assignment area. Col. Edwards became the new battalion commander. Several days passed while other staff and equipment was obtained.

Christmas Day arrived and with it a very decent kitchen to provide us a good meal. Christmas also brought a bit of a snow storm and we had a truly white one. It seems we in S-3 had been out-posted (placed in protective security at some approachable position to the garrison). Though cold, I suggested if someone would obtain a couple of eggs and bag of sugar from the kitchen, I would turn that white stuff into ice-cream. It did transpire, and we were all enjoying our desert until that last bit melted into sort-of clear water to reveal a multitude of very black specks. Shortly however, we were instructed to take control of a small town called Herrlisheim.

The Intelligence passed to us said nothing there but a few old men and a truck or two. This turned out to be a bit inaccurate. Getting in was also complicated by obstacles such as a canal. We did get a few tanks and some Infantry in, but we discovered the Germans had significant infantry, some tanks and anti-tank guns well positioned behind the railroad just east of town.

Capt. Comfort left me his tank and crew to walk into the village to confer with company commanders. Things became quite hot so when the three officers attempted to vacate the building where they had tried to operate as a forward command post. There was an enemy mortar squad setup so close that they heard the shell dropped into the tube and the explosion just outside the door they had just opened. Ultimately, they had to play a timing game; wait for the explosion and immediately run, hopefully before the next shell could be handled. The third man, an infantry lieutenant was injured.

In the meantime, we had been parked alongside a timbered area, later to be known as Steinwald and heavily occupied by German forces. This day we sat there just monitoring radio traffic and what seemed like a small war just a football field away. However, that radio load was our undoing and when Art tried to crank the tank, we didn't have the juice. Well the designer of the Sherman had taken that possibility in mind, so we had what was known as "Little Joe" (a one-cylinder gas engine generator) positioned just to the left shoulder of the loader. Another surprise--it would not start. Fortunately, the radio still had enough kick to summon help and a maintenance man arrived via jeep. He had enough smarts to get "Little Joe" charging.

As it developed, we had just missed our chance to take over Herrlisheim and the German forces were beating us to that punch. In the field we had no knowledge of the battle to our north, nor did we understand the German forces build-up taking place in front of us. Hitler's Bulge failing he had chosen to attempt a break-through where we had been weakened by a stretched front line. This we would later learn he had coded as "Nordwind" and they were in process of assembling two Panzer Divisions and two Infantry Divisions to break out through our thin line to link up with the area they still held at Colmar. My fortunate placement in one of the HQ tanks often left me sitting somewhere short of the hottest action as was the case during most of the month of January 1945. For we had as they say, "a tiger by the tail" at Herrlisheim and were not allowed to give ground. Truth have it, the tigers were shooting us to pieces.

In one attempt at the town we lost an entire Tank Company B. Some of these tanks were captured undamaged, later manned by Germans and used against us. In one day we had 180 men captured including my own Captain Comfort. This is an appropriate moment to note that the two officers who reported to command under the same order as did I are now in command. Col. Edwards is now BTN Commander and Major Schrader is Operations (S3).

At this point I need to reference "A History of the 23rd Tank Battalion" by Jim Francis (see www.12tharmoreddivisionassoc.com). In 2004 when president of the 12th Armored Association, I bemoaned the absence of any publications of battalion exploits and Jim Francis stepped forward. I want to also acknowledge with much gratitude another friend and significant contributor to this referenced publication, Andrew Wood. The stories of these men make my story pale.

Getting back to the passage of time, about January 15th our tank was summoned to take a position alongside a group of A Co. tanks firing as artillery. We were required to elevate the tank by driving the treads up a portion of the rail embankment. This gave our gun adequate elevation to project our fire across the Rhine river. Many years later, in late 1990's, I was discussing history with men in our ADA Reunion and mentioned this occasion but with a question. What were we shooting at? Among us was an A Co. veteran named Walter Breisacher. He said, "Jim, I'll tell you exactly what you were doing."

"You were throwing your shells into a small town where Hitler was amassing his forces to support his desired break through into the Herrlisheim-Camsheim area. You see I am of Jewish decent born in that little village, and as typical we only use one name, but in 1939 we were all being counted and told we had to have a family name and we took the name of the town. Being about 16 at that time my parents sent me out to the US of A. Then I joined the army and so here I am with you and jumping with joy, because you see I knew my family were no more." [end of quote.]

Ultimately with help from the 36th Infantry Div., the breakthrough threat was eliminated about mid-February and our efforts were redirected south toward Colmar to assist the French 1st Army and a Moroccan unit to finally wipe out this German pocket. A minor event this may be, but a not very happy moment. We were traversing an open valley when Art and I looked at each other, for we had both just felt the tank wobble like a car with a loose wheel. We hurried to examine and found the right final drive sprocket very loose. Six of the 12 attachment studs were missing; the remaining six were so loose I literally turned them by hand. We had no tools and I did the best I could do manually. Then Art proceeded to drive carefully out of that valley and into a position where maintenance could take over.

Finally, there was a rest moment and had a few days in Nancy, France for a shower, clean clothes, and a visit to the USO theater. I should be able to tell you who the entertainers were, but I cannot. Just hearing some jokes, looking at pretty girls with lots of leg showing, and knowing this still existed was heart lifting. However, the war was not done contrary to many of those who had celebrated the Normandy Conquest and hedgerow breakout. Even some of the German prisoners we took knew their cause was lost, but Hitler seemed still in command and many clung doggedly to battling.

Joining with Patton

Some, such as Gen. George Patton, knew it was time to take the fight East of the Rhine river. On about March 15th the 12th Armored was summoned by Army command to obliterate unit identity from equipment. Then we were to proceed overnight on a march 100 miles north to Trier. My normal position was still bow gunner, but my secondary position was Assistant Driver and as such I was doing the night driving to allow Art a chance for a few Zee's. We were in column march, immediately behind the battalion commander's tank and in front of him was one light tank. We were moving in secrecy under total blackout conditions. At some point very late in the night our column halted, likely at a road junction. These were always manned by at least some military police.

It was a short sit, probably for directions check, and then I heard the Driver of the light tank clear his engine. My head said to me get ready to move; you know those "cat-eyes" are hard to detect in night conditions. So I leaned into the gearshift to move it into 1st gear. This threw my body forward and down. At that instant a bullet split the air behind my head. Obviously a sniper in the timber some hundred yards to our left had a perfect sighting on my head silhouetted against that moonlit sky. While I am recovering the fright of my life and the wringer squeeze my scalp just gave my skull, the tank behind me did a quick hard left and raked those woods with a burst of machine gun fire. An eerie 20 second disruption in an otherwise soft rumble of a string of tank engines. Later I will say more about this event.

Upon reaching Trier we came under the command of Gen. Patton whose instructions were, "At days light tomorrow I want your entire strike forces driving east at full throttle on all roads to the Rhine." The objective was to skirt or bypass all resistance to seize a bridge hopefully intact and target the town of Worms. The first day out seemed rather quiet; we did have a few surrenders and I acquired my souvenir 32 cal. Mauser pistol. I also learned later that Patton had not been happy with our pace of ground covered.

Surviving Again

At any rate, next day's formation was led off exactly as had been the night march. One Light, the Commander's

Sherman, then our S-3 Sherman, now with all positions as assigned except Maj. Schrader in turret with I thought Col. Edwards. Today we were moving faster, and I occasionally threw some lead in the direction of any movement, always trying to avoid any killing but being sure they were just getting down, not aiming anything. Then we were passing through a very quiet town. Next our road made a rather tight sort of S curve sweeping left around a small hill, then leading to this next town about 150 yards beyond. The column came to an abrupt halt. I never had the opportunity to ask but I believe Lt. Lee in the light tank had spotted motion or a glimmer of light off a gun emplacement. Art had barely completed our turn of the S curve. However, before any words had passed a shell whizzed past in front of us and thudded into the embankment. That was obviously a bad news Armor-piercing shell (no explosion), but to sit there was not smart, so we fired forward hard. The light tank passed through town untouched. Command Tank reached precisely the literal gate of town was hit and stopped. Our tank maybe 30 yards back experienced a loud explosion, shuddered and almost leapt to the right stopping unbelievably fast. In the moment of daze and absence of our officer, though Art was the ranking person, I shouted, "Fellows let's get out of here. I believe we can skirt back around this hill. Basic, in the dirt, knees and elbows," and I lead the way.

Within two minutes the dirt maneuver paid off as machine gun chatter sprayed over us. Now with the uncomfortable thought that capture could be eminent, and wearing a German officer's Pistol belt would not be smart, I deftly unclasped the buckle and crawled beyond the belt.

Gunfire did not last long but abruptly smack in-front of my face was a pair of black boots. As my vision climbed upward, here was an SS officer holding an apparently ready Thompson-type sub-machine gun. He then said, "Surrender Americans, you are my prisoners." Intending to compliment him on his good English I replied in good old army slang, "You sure as hell got that right." Thus, we rose to our feet and were escorted into town and placed in a room of what I judged to be a two-room school building. Was my life coming full circle? I started school in a similar two-room building.

Several other of our troops were added to our quarters. Art had become aware that our loader had been hit with one of those machine gun slugs. The bullet had passed clean through the flesh of his right shoulder and Art was applying a sulfur pack to his wound. We spent the night without food or water, one guard just inside and another just out. They kept a running chatter, probably to verify we had not throttled the guy inside. At one moment they tried to maneuver a truck close to load us in, but thankfully our artillery folk had decided to harass the place with shells. The German troops decided their own escape was primary.

With a short time of peace and quiet, as daylight was just breaking, it was obvious the guards were gone and then we began to detect our infantry were moving into town for the sweep. When I heard one of ours close I opened the door and announced, "only Americans in here." We were pointed the direction back out as they had cleared. As we began to walk out we first observed the Battalion Command Tank with a great gash in the front glacis, that was the mark of a Panzerfaust. This German weapon was a hand held and fired armor-piercing device, similar to our Bazooka and quite effective. However, the strike on the command tank was at an angle too steep to bore through. Had it pierced, there would have been a rain of molten steel in all directions. As it happened, that rain of shrapnel was deadly to the exposed head of the driver and engulfed the area of the commander's open hatch also.

A dozen steps more and we were staring at our own tank. The entire track system on the left was in shambles, but more of a shock to me was the almost 3" hole in the housing of the right final drive gear. This explained the abrupt stop. It also jarred my head with the thought that if that Panzer shot had been just a few inches to the right it would have bored through into <u>ME</u>. [I had hoped to here insert a picture of this tank in the bone yard taken of a maintenance crewman standing just above that welding repair. This man, Calvin Wyese, had been on the retrace 12th Armored tour with me in 1995. When I told this story he said, "Jim I have this photograph because we discussed how we were clad we had not been in your place at that impact." As promised he sent me said photo after we returned. To my carelessness said photo cannot now be found.

At that moment I remembered the souvenir pistol I had left in the field. I turned and took hardly a dozen steps into that field and retrieved my pistol precisely where I had left it.

But moving on back down the tank line, the next one

had taken one of those 88 shells and had burned. By this time, it had quite cooled and I jumped onto the tank and pulled open the driver's hatch. I am still not sure what possessed me to do so, but the gruesome sight cured my curiosity. I then only visually surveyed the field to note about 10 additional tanks in random scatter in a 2-3-acre field.

Art and I continued our march back until we found our forward command post. We received a warm welcome; why not it was two more soldiers they did not have to report dead, injured or missing. In that regard, I am to this day uncertain of the final count. At that moment, they were counting the entire personnel of the Command Tank as dead.

Many years later (1991) I was reporting to my First Annual Reunion, and saw the name Jerome Schrader on the 23rd Battalion roster.

I exclaimed, "This cannot be; we left him for dead at Lohnsfeld."

The attendant replied, "No, Jim, he is here," and rushed off to locate Jerry for me. Shortly they walked up and someone began to introduce us, but Jerry broke in,

"Oh, I certainly remember and recognize Jim."

I said, "Jerry, I'm embarrassed but I had been told you had been finaled."

He replied, "Well the medics and hospital brought me back, but I still carry some souvenir shrapnel and grabbed his neck."

Anyway, back to March 1945. We received some clean-up and feeding It may have been at this time that I had an opportunity to look in a mirror to observe at center of my very dark brown hair was a spot of gray like a silver coin.

Photo 35 years Later

The gray spot did remain a noticeable bit of my hair color until copied by most of the other strands.

New Assignment

Ultimately Art was told he would move to driver of Command Tank with the survivors of both tanks to complete his crew. Actually, the only survivor of that command crew was that young gunner Alvin Wolke who had survived under the collapse of Col. Meigs. But also I would become driver of the S-3 Tank and receive three replacement personnel. It turned out two of them were fresh replacements, but the gunner was an experienced transfer with Buck Sargent stripes. I had just been given T4 stripes which were the norm for my new assignment. Next, I was introduced to 1ˢᵗ Lt. Herman Gerhard who was now the Operations (S3) officer. The two tanks, and many Company A tanks were being repaired or re-serviced for continued action.

Thus, on March 25ᵗʰ I drove LT. Gerhard to the Rhine River just south of Worms where a pontoon bridge was being completed within sight of remains of the Autobahn Bridge. There we met, (correction) Lt. Gerhard met him, I just saw General George S. Patton. I saw him well enough to verify his promised christening of the river. Some readers may not know of this famous quote. Gen Patton, while once addressing the media had said, "When I get to that Rhine I'm going to Piss in it." What I do not recall for certain is whether The General preceded us or otherwise, but we fell in line very early and I drove our refurbished tank across that pontoon bridge.

A few days later we had experienced minor artillery shelling. I don't remember any significant damaging conflicts, but I did witness that our new loader behaved as if in shell shock. The position of loader in the Sherman Tank occupies the left most Turret space, somewhat above and behind the driver. His primary duty is to pull a requested shell from floor rack and place in breach of the big gun. He had spent the entire day and night hovering in his corner of the turret absolutely trembling. The next day I walked into headquarters and ask for audience with the commanding officer. Though not sure who listened to me, my request was for replacement of our Loader as I had to politely declare him unable to function. They did respect my analysis and the replacement was made.

The next couple of days were rather routine for us in S-3. We found very light resistance in Beerfelden and Amorbach. At the end of March we had another fight on our hands. To the best of my knowledge we were parked with a platoon of 23rd tanks just outside Konigshofen. Another of those moments when our officer had dismounted and dashed into the edge of town. As I sat there in daylight hours I happened to observe to our extreme and distant right a German tank emerge from the visible buildings, about to proceed to cross some railroad tracks. The tracks did not run between he and us and thus did not provide him with a defoliate position but might have had he made that crossing. Fortunately, the platoon leader made this same observation and began fire on it. Perfect pattern gunnery our guy fired one short, one over, and next dead on. There was an abrupt flash of fire when that shell hit but in seconds the flames snuffed as though a fire suppression system existed. With that our man pumped in two more rounds and there was nothing more from that tank but flames. I never learned any more of that. However, we were aware our infantry had a building to building fight on their hands and occasionally one soldier would lead a couple of prisoners past our tank. It seemed we were there for the night.

It was certainly not yet warm weather and there was little to warm us in that tank as darkness ascended. My new Assistant driver/bow-gunner was a nice young man of small stature, thus he proceeded to do the almost impossible and place himself into his bedroll right where he was with closed hatch. Little Eddie May was this soldier and I do believe it required at least 20 minutes to achieve his objective. As might be expected, artillery was finally directed at this cluster of tanks. It sounded and felt as though the second round had fallen right on the back deck of our tank. I quickly adjudged it had not set us aflame but by the time I looked at Eddie he was no longer in a bedroll. The harassing fire did not last long; our Lt. Gerhard returned and we cleared the area. This as it turned out was our closest approach toward Berlin.

Our next orders were to turn south to sweep the Bavarian area. At about this moment in time Lt. Gerhard came to me and said Jim we are to go back and get a new tank. I don't even remember if our other crew went, but I drove us back over that same pontoon bridge and traded the old beat-up M4 for a brand new M4a3e8, then crossed the Rhine for our third time. By this time, it was early April and weather was improving as were our spirits. There were small skirmishes, but mostly it was checking surrenders for weapons and pointing them rearward. It suddenly occurred to me I was seeing much less of Art Ostergaard and the Commander's Tank crew. I had surmised that this was to reduce that chance of losing two ranking officers by one shot again. It may have had more to do with the sweeping action which now involved our entire division. We have from the beginning operated as three Combat Commands, CCA, CCB, & CCR. This R command was generally 23rd Tank, 17th Infantry, & 495th Field Artillery. So even though I had not had this explained, I had to assume we were sweeping via three separate roads and the new battalion commander, had assigned S3 officer Gerhard to lead CCR while he remained close to Division HQ, for coordination.

At the outset of this sweep, we did not find much resistance and would generally park for the night in the last town we had claimed that day. One day found us on a trail, much like just a logging trail, through a wooded area and low and behold we came upon a typical VW auto stopped by a fair-sized puddle where a small stream crossed the road. It really was blocking the path. I think even before the lieutenant spoke any orders, I said to our crew that I bet if we all search the area, that key is lying where the driver pitched it. Sure enough, one of them found it in less than two minutes. I told him to get in and crank it. When it responded beautifully, I told him to not to spin wheels but just help as we other three pushed. It walked right out. So then I addressed Lt. Gerhard and said, "Sir, if we let him bring it along you could have wheels tonight." His response, "Have him bring it along at the back of the Column." He continued saying, "clear enough side space for you and him and to allow the column to pass." He then instructed the section leader to proceed cautiously in event there were armed enemy in front.

All continued for a half hour or so and "Sir Herman" said, "they have seen something. I need to get up there." I said, "Brace yourself, we will proceed for a new path, picking my trees, ones I could just walk up to and brute down." In short order, we were back in front and the two officers conferred. I never observed any threat; it may have been a direction thing for we were soon back on a better road. We did find a town to settle in that night with more of the CCR soldiers. The car seemed to disappear, perhaps commandeered by someone with more "shoulder brass."

More Surprises

My next adventure seemed similar as we were again proceeding on a typically narrow road, but again with the Company of tanks ahead. Then Gerhard received a call to come forward. He told the platoon leader to tell his drivers to pull as hard right as possible, then instructed me to drive forward past all of them. As we reached the point of the column we had come upon a "T" intersection but dead in front of us was a prison type fenced compound. Right over the gate, also just a mix of chicken wire and barbed wire, a sign read "Dachau." Lt. Gerhard said, "Jim put this tank through that gate." Big Shermie had no problem and soon that gate was flat under us.

I had barely stopped and Gerhard dismounted and headed to a concrete building on our right. Just this side of the building was a huge stack of bodies, now just skeletons. You see we were not at the site of a massive prisoner encampment; we were at the extermination site. Looking back in front, here came a man toward me, one of those still walking skin & bones. I was just about to panic with thought—what would, what could I do. But still 40-50 feet away he was just too exhausted to make it and he sat down on a large stone. Also at that moment Lt. Gerhard was back on the tank and said, "Jim, I have called for the medics; we don't belong here, let's get out.." Just intuitively, I backed left to give us an effective right turn on the road we had just intersected. So we moved

40

out, now leading. For those who may have researched extermination camps, you will read that the Dachau gas chamber had never been used. Unfortunately, I was not able to photograph this view, but there was certainly a reason for the stack of emaciated bodies just outside the building. Reports do say many died there of the brutal experiments by T4 medical doctors.

It turned out we were only about 12 miles from Munich and we shortly intersected a superhighway such as I had never seen. This road lead straight into Munich and had two wide lanes each way with a divider between. Obviously, an effective air strip and we were privileged to see the planes pushed tail first back into the woods. Some of the exact detail has left me but as I recall my tank was parked as though ready to leave the outskirts of Munich. Just off highway to my left was a row of what I call hedge trees, maybe 15-20 feet tall. As per normal the Lt. had walked away. We and other tanker men were lounging, I on the back deck with my back against the turret. Shortly we heard an engine like the engine of a small plane crank up on the far side of that hedge row. I jumped to my feet and sure enough right across the trees from me rose this single engine unmarked light plane. With the 50-cal. machine gun practically in my hands, I loaded a round into the chamber and swung it at the plane, pulled the trigger, and fired about five rounds watching the last two go into the engine cowling. That was the last because the Ammo belt was empty, had been neglected. I have had trouble with this, believing some ranking enemy person had escaped his due. Then a preacher in my church stated the profound, "Jim, just as those earlier rounds had not found you, perhaps it was not yet his time either."

As per the calendar, this was about day one of May 1945, but we still had assigned areas SW of Munich to clear. So we moved onward toward Austria. About May 3 we reached the town of Kufstein, Austria. The next day we were to hand over care of this area to the 36th Infantry Div. and we to assemble back north of the Danube river at Heidenheim. I probably did leave early that day for Heidenheim. However, before all our battalion had left Kufstein there was this bit of action I must tell. We of the 23rd Tank call this "The Adventure at Itter Castle."

On May Fourth, a German Wehrmacht Major drove into Kufstein with a white flag attached to his *Kubelwagen* (similar to a Jeep). He said he could take us to 14 French notables who had been hiding in an old castle. Several had once been part of the French government before the Germans invaded France in 1940. There was also a large force of German troops with them who wished to surrender.

Itter Castle Adventure

This lead to the last battle, on this front, but a story worthy of a Hollywood movie. Captain John Lee was commanding Company B of the 23rd Tank and took on this job even though the 36th infantry had "officially" relieved our division. He and the German major drove a few miles south of Kufstein to confirm the Offer. Differing reports say a German colonel refused to surrender, but is unclear if he commanded Wehrmacht troops or the SS troops who were laying siege on the castle.

German troops in Worgl apparently did surrender. Explosives under a bridge leading into Worgl were removed, and ammunition for antitank guns was taken away. The SS troops at Itter, however, were still trying to get to the French big-wigs holed up in the castle.

Captain Lee went back to Kufstein and got together a small task force, largely volunteers. It was his own tank and crew, Company B's motor officer, 1st Lt. Harry Basse, in another tank with a voluntary crew, and about a half dozen Infantry men from Company D of 17th AIB who agreed to ride on the back decks of the two tanks. (D17 AIB was an all-black unit and many were eager to show they were the equal of any soldier.) In addition, five tanks and crews from the 36th Infantry came with them.

At Worgl, only the two tanks of Company B went with their infantry men into town, while the others stayed out. One tank and three infantry men stayed in Worgl to clear the area, take prisoner any Germans they encountered, and guard the bridge. Tech. Sargent Elliot was in charge of this group and Lt. Basse joined Captain Lee's crew. Then only the one tank and its three-man infantry support went on to Itter.

They ran into SS troops on the road and had to shoot their way through to get to the Castle. The tank was parked blocking the entrance into the castle grounds and the shooting continued. Lee's group defended themselves with the tank cannon, the machine guns and the infantry's M-1 rifles. The SS soldiers had an antitank gun, though, and they knocked out the tank and set it on fire. Lee's eight men survived and ran back into the castle.

Sure enough, the French notables were really there—former premiers, generals, political leaders, wives, and a French tennis star. Also, there were a dozen Wehrmacht soldiers commanded by a Major. The Major offered to help defend the castle and it's occupants. Captain Lee agreed and the German soldiers took up firing positions at the windows. The only means of communication from the castle was by phone and of course that did not reach Lee's Volunteers waiting in and beyond Worgl.

For sixteen hours through the night and the next morning, the siege by the SS continued. Tragically some of the Wehrmacht soldiers and their commander were killed in the long fight. The "rear guard" at Worgl finally decided to wait no longer and came to the rescue. Approaching the castle, they heard the sound of an American machine gun (much slower than the German Burp gun) and knew Lee's group were inside. Faced with six tanks, the SS troops soon put up their hands in surrender. The castle was freed at about 3:00 in the afternoon. Several jeeps were brought up to the castle as transportation for the famous French folk. Lee and his heroes, though, had to ride back to Kufstein in a truck with the prisoners.

Missions Accomplished

Thus ended combat for the 23rd Tank Battalion and all of the 12th Armored Division. Our Division was assigned a large area for security and occupation duties. Division HQ was located in Heidenheim, 15 to 20 miles northwest of Dilligen where we had crossed the Danube River less than two weeks earlier.

Anyway, I had not even settled until Lt. Gerhard came up to us and said, "Fellows we seem to be sitting too low in this valley and our communications group cannot talk with HQ. Thus, I am sending you out onto the hill to act as guard for the radio crew in their half-track." Lt. might have been inclined to bust my butt, but I told his Jeep driver to stay out from under my tracks, for I was going to see how fast this tank was. When we reached the village on the hill, we were being offered nice quarters in the guesthouse.   Unfortunately, even there the radio crew reported poor communications and we had to relocate on the hill above their little lake. The jeep driver reported our top speed had been about 31 MPH. We were there probably less than a week with our tank crew of four rotating guard alert while the radio crew also rotated their duty. Sleeping in our vehicles meant we were little better than we had been during action days. However, not one time was there any hostile action or unpleasant moments. In fact, since it had become very pleasant weather, the little lake became the local swimming hole and the young girls seemed to make a point of entertaining us.

However, back at HQ, the staff with other duties had been counting point status to see who would go home, who would have more permanent occupation duty, and who, such as I, would be sent to help end the war persisting in the Pacific. While awaiting more definitive orders we could stroll through local communities. Usually it was wise to be in groups or at least two, so one day a friend and I were on one of these strolls. We had hardly become aware of an encampment of Russian troops about 100 yards off the road to our right when a bullet whistled over our heads. The lad with me, perhaps bigger and gutsier, said, "Let's go." He bypassed the language barrier by pulling that rifle from the hands of the young Russian, stripped the bolt, threw it to the ground then thrust the weapon back into his hands. This was my one encounter with Russian troops and was perhaps somewhat less than wise. After all we were just two and the Russian encampment were not a happy lot.

Though it now seems a long gap between late May and mid-August it holds little interest beyond those efforts to be transported. By mid-August we were well on our way to re-crossing the Atlantic. On August 14th President Harry Truman gave me a birthday present when he committed the atomic bombs to end that war. Thus, our ship destined toward the Panama Canal was now rerouted to Boston Harbor where we debarked to a glorious celebration.

Chapter Three

POST WAR YEARS

WITH GOVERNMENT TRANSPORT BACK TO Camp Grant in Chicago, I was shortly on leave to a family reunion. At home to the Wood-River/Wanda area, I found with a little surprise that my family were no longer on the farm. My parents had purchased a location in WR which had only a two-car garage and were living elsewhere in rented space, with plans for building a home. Where they were living, I joined them in the upper floor of the historic home place of the Roseberry family. Living there on the main floor were the two aunts of Gordon Roseberry who had married my sister Cleta. They were the widowed Mrs. Nettie Ryan and her sister Ruby Roseberry.

I did make at least one trip to Louisville and recall I did in fact bring Lady-Jane home to meet and have a short visit with my family.

Jane & I again with '40 Ford

However, at this moment I did not have a Discharge and was obliged to return to Grant for another six-month duty before the Army released me. So, about March 1946, I was home with Discharge in hand, finding a couple of my closest friends at home, but not released from Marine Corps. They were merely in reserve status with week-end duty at St. Louis Airport as ground crew for a Squad of Vaught F-4U Corsair Air-Wing Pilots to maintain flight proficiency. They said, "Hey Jim, it's fun duty and with a little pay. Come with us." I walked into the Marine Office with my discharge, they gave me a uniform with three stripes, and for a year I was a week-end Marine.

Our plane & pilot
Me on wing

A New Family Home

During the week I was, you might say, repaying Dad
for that several months of having his auto at Fort Knox for
getting to know the girls in Louisville. However, now we
had a house to build. With new obligations, the visits to
Louisville were losing priority and there were after all local
ladies, though most that I had known were now married.
The subject of marriage was not yet appropriate for a guy
with little income and aspirations for college on the GI
bill. I had just applied for admission to The University of
Illinois (U of I), to study Mechanical Engineering and had
enrolled at the local junior college, for prep-engineering.

The house construction had turned into quite a
challenge as the only dimension lumber available was oak.
Maybe it had been Dad's plan (or then became the plan) to

make a small attachment to the garage to accommodate till better lumber would allow building the home up front of the lot. But cutting and nailing had begun, and that fresh oak was presenting the expected challenge. Dad and I looked at each other and agreed, "I hope I never have to take this apart."

By the end of summer, we had a cozy four-room cottage with restroom in half the garage. Marine duty had also occupied me, but somewhere along my close friends had appealed for me to join them and their lady friends for an evening dinner boat cruise. I protested, "Fellows I have no date." Donald Wood had met and dated a young lady and said she has a sister. Thus, somehow, I became acquainted with the pretty lady then known as Alice Horstman. And yes, about two years later that lady, became Mrs. Feezel. I should add that I had used the defense, "but she was so pretty and I could not forget her birthday." (It was the same as mine.)

With the small house up and occupied, the Summer of 1947 was less busy and our air wing was scheduled to a two-week training trip to El Toro Marine Base at Long Beach California. This became another blessing because I had long had an uncle, Harry Eyestone, residing in the Long Beach area. This allowed me to visit with him and my cousins, at their lush little fruit and vegetable farm. The fruit trees were a special excitement as I had never before experienced most of this. When I returned from our mission to El Toro I found that I had a letter from the U of I telling me I had been accepted to begin with the fall term. I next walked into the Marine HQ and told them I would be unable to maintain my status with them due to being at Urbana-Champaign, Illinois, thus requesting discharge which was granted.

Off to College

One of my close friends, Gene Knipping had also received his Acceptance and in our searches for living quarters we finally booked a tiny apartment in a private boarding house where our rent was paid by our basic maintenance of the upper dormitory. I probably never heard all the reasons for Gene's departure, but by the end of that first year, he reported that he was quitting. Sure enough, he returned home and married his girl.

Having been also less than totally enthused with the living and working facilities, I did more scouting and found a similar rental plan at another and nicer private home owned and managed by a widowed lady. So the year 48-49 progressed well enough and my lady Alice had spent the year working for Bell Telephone Co. in her Hometown, Alton IL. With one year left to finish my degree I approached my landlady on possibility of returning in the fall with a wife and maintaining some similar contract with her. We then made an agreement wherein I added maintenance of the stoker feed furnace and she granted us kitchen privileges. Needless to say, I had managed to scrape up enough to obtain an engagement ring which Alice had accepted the summer of 1948. That had carried the plan to marry in June of '49.

Thus began our whirlwind summer of 1949. I was still without wheels of my own; those of you with history of that subject will remember there had been no auto production From February 1942 to October 1945. In spring of 1949 I still did not have the price nor the ability to get on the list for these warmed over 1942 models. To begin some separation of my life from the total distraction of my parents or other family, I needed wheels. More on this shortly. Alice and I did marry in June despite a tornado having struck the town of WR that produced minor damage to my parents' home and to the home of my sister Cleta and her husband.

The girl I married

Wedding Couple

That tornado is quite a story itself and occurred while Cleta & Gordon, Alice & I were in St. Louis shopping for Wedding needs. It also caused the destruction of much of my Military Memorabilia. This consisted mostly of the correspondences between my folks and I plus other wartime mail from such as Lady Jane.

Wartime production had shutdown automobile production which had not yet resumed. Used vehicles were scarce, but low and behold one, a 1937 Plymouth coupe had been left sitting on concrete blocks in a field of the farm that my sister Louise and her husband Norman Klueter had recently purchased. The legal acquiring of title became a story in its own. Skip that, it was achieved and with scarce dollars and loving work Alice and I refurbished said vehicle. By September we had a reasonably respectable vehicle to carry Alice and I to our living in Campaign, IL.

Alice was also able to negotiate a transfer with Illinois Bell which gave her employment there. If you like history, check out "telephone switchboard operators." Invented in 1876, Bell Telephone Co. began a year later, and in 1947 and later it still employed people like Alice to connect one person to the next. As for today, we carry the total communication system in our pocket or purse. Well, we still need those linking cellular towers.

Be that as it may, our life was progressing. I had much work to do at the University and at our living quarters. I was within walking distance of Engineering Campus, but Alice needed transport and mostly drove. I shortly discovered an advertised "Immaculate 1940 Old's Coupe" for sale. I bought the Old's and sold my Plymouth to an Iranian prince in Liberal Arts school. That Plymouth was then all over town with him and no less than two ladies at a time.

However, Alice was soon to discover she had fallen victim of that age old feminine malady "morning sickness." God saw us through it all and by May we graduating engineers were having opportunities to interview with visiting employers and one of my interviews found pay dirt.

<u>Graduate's New Job</u>

I was given a precious offer with Diamond Chain Co. in Indianapolis, Indiana. Graduation was a great celebration, though some discomfort for my wife. Soon

I was returning my expectant wife with her parents in Alton, Illinois and I was off to Indianapolis.

In this time of whirlwind events I do not recall the sequencing, but I guess apartment hunting came first. As I made my appointed date at Diamond Chain and sat with the Personnel Director who had hired me, his phone rang. With proper apology he turned to answer, but when he turned back, with a smile on his face he said, "Young man, go home, you have a son." Then he said, "Let me be the first to congratulate you; take a week and come back to see me." Maybe it was two weeks maybe more, but eventually the family of now three (with son Richard) were back and moving into our small apartment. Our widowed landlady had developed one as part of her first floor adjacent to her kitchen and living rooms.

Now at work, I discovered the Engineering Department to be housed in one rather large room, reminiscent of a classroom with the chief's desk placed like a teacher's desk. There were three sections staffed in three rows. I was at the back of the center row of five. We were the Research and Development team. The chief spent time with me, teaching me to read finished part surface hardness with a machinist file. We used lots of files because once used on the hard parts they also changed character. Many of our product components were cylindrical parts roll-formed from strip steel. The chief had assigned me the task of developing a tighter closure of that seam. We had achieved some success by just rattling the parts against each other in a tumbling drum, and I was researching a procedure of peening with fine steel shot.

On the personal side, just one and a half years in Indianapolis, we were now four with a son and a daughter, Jeanette Alyece. I needed to think house. One of the shop foremen I had come to know helped me to find a farmer who would sell me an acre strip with access to a secondary road. The other man hired from the U of I had arrived in town with two young daughters. When he heard me discussing house building he said, "Jim, I could not build a house, but I sure would help you if we could agree to build two." We agreed; Bill Barber bought-in half the piece of ground and we started my house. I mean we built from ground up—trenched, poured footing, laid block, then all the lumber work. By Christmas 1951 we moved into our new home.

First Home
Brownsburg, IN

By Winter of 1952 the Barber family were in their home as well. There were several unforgettable instances in these projects. Perhaps the very first was that Saturday in the summer of 1951. With just sub floor down, most of the engineering department staff appeared on site for a fantastic day of wall raising. Then while I was working alone one evening to install air system ducting, I made a bad lift, resulting in a slipped sacrum. I managed to drive home and crawl into bed. However, next AM I could not get out. Our landlady said, "No problem, you are in the chiropractic capitol of the world." She called the school, who sent out a graduate student. He checked me and the bed, took Alice's one-piece ironing board, slipped it between the mattress and springs, put me in pretzel hold and snapped me back into good shape. Then asked, "Can you get up?" I answered by swinging my legs off the bed and stood up.

The third instance, one fine spring Saturday I was at the Barber house; walls were up and we were placing ceiling joists. My access ladder was leaning against the back wall of the framing. I sensed motion, looked over and discovered my two-year-old son about to crawl from the ladder onto the recently placed ceiling joists. His desire to learn had started very early. Naturally I scrambled to quickly meet him at that point and with him in arms, I told him what I was doing on top of that unfinished building. Then we adjourned to our own home for an evening snack and bedtime.

The sad part of having built our two homes in such short time at Diamond Chain was to follow. Bill who had been working in tool design, had received an offer of employment at a tool manufacturing firm within a year of having occupied his home. Then, while having thanksgiving holiday with my parents in Illinois, I was told by my dad that the refinery was looking for engineers. I rang the phone of the Chief Engineer; a hasty interview was arranged and I received an offer with significant pay increase. After completing our contracted notice time, Bill and I both left Diamond Chain after little more than three years.

A Company Career

However, I now was working for a much larger company, Standard oil of Indiana, and in my home town. Now we had two daughters plus the sparkling son. Again, a home was needed. This time I found a builder near my rental home, drew up my plan, and negotiated with him to construct the house to the point of dry-in. I then proceeded with interior, subcontracting major plumbing, but doing all electrical, the heat system, and interior finish. This home I designed with radiant heated ceilings with controlled temp water from oil fired boiler. I am now uncertain when I met the gentleman, but when we joined the St. John's Methodist Church in Edwardsville near our new home, the teacher of the adult class that Alice and I attended was indeed in the business of selling these radiant systems. We became good friends. I probably should also mention that the one-acre plot of ground I acquired was very near my Sister Cleta and her husband, Gordon. Their son, Larry was just three years older than my son Richard and the boys did share much time together.

Home #2
Edwardsville, IL

At this point in my life we are in year 1954. I am approaching the end of my 20's and busy raising a family; still I found time for a civic duty. I became a member of the group known as Wood-River Junior Chamber of Commerce. Memories are scant but several years into this experience I was elected President and do remember that year we conducted a driver education and talent program for high school aged youngsters. We arranged with the local Bethalto Regional Airport for use of a large section of parking area to set-up obstacle courses and parking challenges. We awarded some prizes as incentive to participation.

One other event that has remained vivid was this. In our regular meetings, we often sang an appropriate Christian song. Apparently, my voice had been noted (loudly). A good friend standing near-by explained, "Well, his church lets him sing." Perhaps also it should have been a wake-up that my ears had been damaged in 1944-45. The good friend near-by was a gentleman named Roger Harris. He had received his engineering degree from The Rolla School of Mines in Missouri, and had started work at Standard Oil on precise schedule with mine.

As for plant duty, it seemed we all started as inspectors for safety and hazards, but then moved into operational or functional problem solving. A few years into my work, the plant section known as Light Oils requested an engineer placed directly in their department for more direct coordination. I was given this duty assignment. I do not recall many of our projects, but it seems I was invited for suggestions and recommendations. Thus, one day I advised that one difficulty at the Poly-butane Plant to produce at specification was the slow gravitational separation of catalyst from product. I stated that if desired and development funds were provided I would work with a manufacturer to design a machine to correct this. Ultimately, and on a test slip stream we produced some of the highest quality product ever tested. Then in cooperation with our legal department a patent was granted in my name. Naturally the application patent was owned by the company. No one ever handed me a big check, but I kept my job and pay raises did occur. Not that I was the only one, but at my 10th anniversary, the Company did present me with a small pin in the Standard logo design with a small diamond. The company I went to work for was one of the several companies generated when the U.S. government, in 1911, decided that the Rockefeller Oil Business operating as Standard Oil was an illegal monopoly. Most of them merely added the label "of ------" (which was the State where their Major Refinery operated.) Our senior and major refinery was in Whiting, Indiana though our Corporate Headquarters was in Chicago. Through the dozen years I worked in Illinois the name did change—next to American Oil and then to Amoco Oil.

A New Opportunity

Then in about my 13th year, Amoco announced they were going to add a Chemical division and would build a plant in Decatur, Alabama. I approached the Chief Engineer and stated I wanted to volunteer for a position at the Decatur Site. Their immediate answer was we will send you, for a year's learning to our Joliet, Illinois sight where production had just grown past the research and development state. Here I met William H. Lovin who had been hired as a native Alabamian, also at Joliet to learn the business.

We settled our family into a unique rental property. This house had developed in stages by a self-employed carpenter; he lived in another of his products but seemed never to find the end of this one. Including the basement, it had five levels, with a master bedroom that could almost function as a stand-alone apartment. This put Alice and I on the third floor with our youngest daughter also in a separate room, near us. The older three girls were on the 4th level in two bedrooms, and our son had the 5th level alone (we called it penthouse). I believe all the children will have memories of this year, I hope mostly pleasant, but also should let them edit this last paragraph for accuracy.

There was a lake or pond nearby and I think by November was frozen well enough for Ice-skating. Alice was quite accomplished at this sport and soon had all five of the youngsters enjoying this. It was well that they had this diversion because I was spending most all my daylight hours at the plant. Alice with what the older three contributed had to manage house, food and all.

Spring arrived and with it the tornadoes. One day at the plant we received the warning of one headed our way. We in front office were advised that our best hope was under our heavy desks. However, I first walked to the front door to spot the monster and appraise its intent. Surely enough it seemed bent on a perfect path at our building, but as I watched and debated, the funnel contacted the line of power poles bringing that energy to our plant. The funnel turned squarely north with that line of power poles and was picking each one out of the ground and flinging them like toothpicks. I was spared the crouch under my desk, but the city north of our plant did receive residential and perhaps other damage. Our neighborhood was further north and spared this time. Later that evening, I had just retired to my bed and another warning came. Alice the good mother, gathered her flock and headed to the basement. I however, rather exhausted declined, saying "I am too tired, maybe it will just take bed and all and let me down softly." I literally slept through the storm and it only claimed our trash cans, but did quite serious damage to the home across our street. As I recall such events, I am aware today I am almost totally deaf without hearing equipment. In that year and perhaps self-trained at lip-reading, I did not wear hearing aids. Perhaps someone "upstairs" listened for me.

When we had left our home at Edwardsville, I was committed to this move and had placed the property for sale with a Realtor. When home for Christmas Holiday, the place had not sold but the most interested family had been headed by a horticulturist. I decided this was a God send, to myself. "Remember you had planted all those fruit trees and berry vines, because you like fruit, but have no such ability." I rang up the gentleman, invited him to a re-look and discussion. His name was Chris Dohl and he was employed by the County Agricultural Dept. We made an agreement and he turned it into a beautiful orchard. With relatives nearby, I did not lose contact and have more than once had opportunity to eat delicious peaches grown on trees I had planted. "Life is wonderful!"

Southern Migration or Decatur Decisions

By the time the school year ended I had met the gentleman assigned to be Manager at the Decatur site. His name was Paul Lamont and he had the final authority on staffing the Decatur site. He ultimately agreed to my position as Staff Engineer but that I would begin site duty when the Chicago construction engineers were on site. Since the status in June 1965 was still in land grading stage, I was farmed back to Wood River engineering for their needs and told to make an exploratory trip to Decatur for residence need.

Bill Lovin had arranged for me to meet there with a prominent Realtor for assistance. The predominant logic was this individual should be located east of Sixth Avenue. There was no adequate available home and very limited construction sites. The "Belt-line Road" which would be our prominent path to plant site was just then also in grading state. The area just north and east of the Belt was rather alive with home construction contractors. Here I found a contractor with two four-bedroom homes under construction on Azalea Circle. We looked at both, discussing prices, and then he said I have an interested party who said he will want one of these, and gave me the name, Al Ruscilli. I laughed a bit and told him that since that gentleman is to be my immediate boss the decision is made; I'll take the choice he leaves.

Decisions were soon made, and my wife had the opportunity to make some flooring decisions and color choices. Even I knew these were matters best left to the ladies. Then with a pleasant summer in Hometown we were back as family to sign papers assign room spaces and register students into another new school. My son found himself as sophomore in the brand-new Austin High. On that first visit while traveling from the belt-line up Westmead St., we noted a building going up very near the Austin High, and I asked what is that to be. "Oh, that is a Methodist Church" came the answer. My response, well there is another Provident Grace. I have been a Methodist my entire life and my Presbyterian wife, though we married in her church, has yielded to my choice. Indeed, we had been an active family in St. John's United Methodist Church in Edwardsville for some dozen years. Thus, in the Fall we walked into the freshly occupied Wesley United Methodist Church with its currently small membership We have since joked, "that day we doubled their membership." Well we must be forgiven once in a while. We found here many wonderful people. Please forgive any omissions but certain ones came to mind: Quitman Henderson, Austin High Principal, his wife a teacher Ann Henderson, and Helen Thompson, pianist / organist for many years, and also a teacher. Alice found the Choir and never let go until her final day.

Thus settled in, I literally dug into bringing the Amoco Decatur plant out of the ground. Yes, with much help, this may not be an exact count, but we had at least four contract companies, probably 100 engineers from home office, and maybe a dozen local hires to inspect or at least observe the progress. I was functioning out of a trailer following utilities construction. With completion of the Main Office Building and as other permanent staff did so, I moved into one of the engineering offices. Shortly it was time to accept various elements of the utility systems. A young man named Buck Isabel had been hired from somewhere in Texas to be Operating Supervisor of Utility Facilities. I worked closely with Buck as water treatment, cooling towers, waste treatment, and then boilers were brought up. About three years later, I was told Buck would be going back to Texas City and I would be promoted to Operations Supervisor for management of Utilities Systems. After several years as Utilities Super I moved throughout the plant as Operations Super of most units, but especially the primary oxidation plants.

International Adventures Again

Also over these years Amoco Chemical was building a facility in Virginia and Joint ventures in other countries. I believe it was the Fall of 1973 I was sent to Gael, Belgium because our facility there was having problems with waste treatment. After a few weeks there, I requested to take a two-week vacation tour of Europe. This had been my first opportunity back to that area since my war days in France and Germany. The young lady at the plant switchboard spoke perfect English and had command of seven languages. I cannot even name all of them. When I told her my plan and purpose, with the several names I could recall, she mapped a route for myself and Alice, who had been allowed to accompany me on this assignment.

We started this vacation with a slip into Holland to Amsterdam, but misfortune met us there when our parked Auto was broken into. They took my briefcase and camera case; however, I did have the camera on me. So I did get some great pics. Then we went on to Trier, Bohmholder, and others. I had intended to drive to Kufstein, Austria, but at the border could not produce my Green Card. Lost with that brief case, we had to turn back. Probably good luck since it was rainy and Austria can be treacherous. We reversed into Munich, found a *Gausthausen* for a bed and some chow. The dining chamber was packed but the maître de approached two ladies in a booth and they graciously agreed for us to join them. They handled some English, I handled very little German, but we had fun.

Soon however, we were back in Decatur and at the routine grind of keeping Terephthalic Acid production high. At this time, we had retired and torn down the First Oxidation Unit, but it had long since been replaced by numbers three and four. Amoco was ready to launch Oxy #5 with #5 PTA. The Oxidation Plant process involves catalytic addition of oxygen to a Xylene to render Terephthalic Acid. The PTA plants increase the purity of the specific acid to a 99.9% level. I followed the building and then started up the #5 Oxidation Plant. In these late units centrifuges were used to separate the slurry liquor from the product powder and a lot of maintenance was required to keep many of these machines operational. This may have had something to do with the move, but I was tagged to transfer into the Maintenance Department. Once there and managing this aspect of maintenance, I set up a program of identification of each machine and each gearbox with a servicing program to minimize the outage of these critical units.

With a busy work life and raising the five children,

our kids, 2015

of whom we were quite proud, by 1976 only one was still at home and in High School. I chose to build one more house. After selecting and obtaining the lot, I established the ground limits and gave Alice the pencil to design her house. I had an Architect turn it into building plans. Again, this time I used a contractor to bring it to "weather-in." (An interesting note here; the contractor who had built my parents' home in WR after 1946 had come to Alabama and I had him build this house. Thus, just before Christmas of '76 we moved to 2804 Wayne Dr. in Decatur.

Third built Home
Decatur, AL

I may not be remembering why I was visiting my home area around Thanksgiving without Alice and Deb but I was, and decided to take back a new car for Alice. So, I bought a pretty Blue Buick Regal from the dealer in Edwardsville and drove it home to Her. I am sure she was thrilled, but some while later she confessed "what I really would love to have is the Oldsmobile Tornado." It may have been a couple years later while visiting Irby Johnson, car dealer and co-founder of Wesley that I spoke about my wife wanting a tornado. He said, "I have a beauty on the back lot, let me bring it around." Another beautiful blue (to match her eyes) with a Stainless top. So yes, she had her Tornado.

Also about this time, the year 1978, a friend and I had discussed maybe retiring to our own business. He approached me with, "I have just spoken with Don Bowden and I believe we should start up a solar energy business." Donald R. Bowden had initiated his company, Solar Unlimited, in 1976 and our plan was to install systems of Don's Design along with our other work. It was like the company was listening. They called me to the office to tell me they needed me to go to Mexico to pick up the job of plant start-up because our man there had become quite ill and must come home. We left Deb with a small Toyota to get to school and brought Alice's mom and Dad to the house (to limit damages).

Once there we were in the process of test operation of utilities systems and I had an experienced Decatur Utilities Foreman to help me. Boiler start-up had progressed to the point we were bringing up the turbine driven centrifugal air compressor. Late that evening a loss of load allowed the compressor to over-speed with catastrophic result. Turbine wheel disintegrated and ruptured the cast housing. My U.S. experience and data indicated a probable six-week delay to obtain new cast housing and wheel. The attendant explosive exhaust of steam also overtaxed the boiler surge resulting in collapse of a super-heater baffle. This was another major work project. Then the Mexican workers blew my mind. They welded the pieces of that cast housing back in place and another welder, lying on his back working through a 1-1/2" drain plug, forced the 14" diameter baffle into place and welded it. I chose not to stand in that turbine room for the next start-up, but it held the 500 lb. pressure and was successful.

Within about a three-month period we deemed the utilities systems operational and I returned to Decatur plant while other personnel assisted start-up of the Oxidation Plant. However, in 1977 centrifuges failures were harming operations and I was sent back to instruct and guide the maintenance staff to the proper care of those machines. This tour also required some reorganization of spare parts supplies and extended for most of that year.

With less than a year back at work in Decatur, our company was committing assistance on the Island of Trinidad for construction and start-up of an ammonia plant. I again received a call to assume our duties as regarded utilities systems. Thus, in November 1979, Alice and I packed our bags for a long stay on the Island of Trinidad. This project was in initial stages of construction. We met with the native personnel who would man the operating plant, and began to monitor construction. It was just out of one of these meetings that the Amoco Manager collared me and with some emphasizing profanity said, "Jim, go get a hearing aide." My deficiency was impeding, so now began my search for adequate hearing support. Meanwhile, I did help train boiler operators, designed pipe flushing projects, and generally brought up the utilities systems.

It took us a little over a year but about march of '81 we had brought it on line and had a Grand Open House. This had been an interesting and rewarding job. Almost before we had settled-in we met and became friends with Mr. and Mrs. Lou Hurrell who were on the Island with their two children. Lou was a retired RAF pilot now hired to train native pilots for capability to land the commercial aircraft on the island's limited Runway. We had beach side picnics with this family and took some week-end excursions to other Caribbean Islands with them. When Alice later injured her foot, the daughter Karen spent time with us to tend chores for Alice. The Plant Manager had rented a string of new apartments just off the road into the plant to have several of us close because the highway from Port-of-Spain was heavily loaded and took more than an hour in the morning to reach the plant. This placed us at the very witness point of the sugar cane field burn-off. It also had us close to witness the burnout and collapse of the power line into our plant. During a midnight windstorm the lines whipped together and with no line breakers in place the lines melted themselves off the poles. Quite a fourth-of-July type wake-up.

Time for Second Career

In the spring of '82 I was home at my Maintenance Supervisor job for a short time, but my planning friend was then assigned to a job in Taiwan. In early 1983 Amoco was negotiating to sell the chemical business to British Petroleum. So they offered many of us a retirement plan and many accepted [including myself]. Then Mr. Tomas Dill and I did crank up Solar-Matic Co. This venture was largely unsuccessful, but we did learn some lessons and I did solar-ize my Decatur home.

Finally I could take more time to work for my church and I spent several years in or chairing Trustees. I had signed up for membership in Trustee Committee in '83 and clearly remember at the first meeting someone explained it was their policy to elect their own chairmen and I think it was J.K. Howard who nominated me and then closed the nominations. I protested they should allow me a year's understudy, but they liked the gamble. J.K. and I became great friends and worked many small projects, many like the Sanctuary side indirect lighting built in his home shop. We did accomplish a couple small additions and when we found a good speaker we managed to get the parking lot paved. I wish I could remember that man's name. In my half century at Wesley I have known so very many bright and talented people, many of them necessarily have moved on. I believe it was in '84 Bill Morgan was our minister and we were discussing the need to pave a dirt parking lot. Mr. Morgan allowed that since the budget was inadequate we might appeal on Sunday directly for a special funding. This young gentleman volunteered to be spokesperson. So, when announced on Sunday, he entered by the back side door, dressed in a suit covered in dust, (chalk, that is) and made our pitch. We paved the lot.

With more time to travel and having been told the farm home of my youth had been moved but still existed, I scouted. It turned out a state plan to revise a flood plain and move a levee wall would encompass the small farm. The house was sold and moved approx. 1/2 mile and over the very elevated railroad which was a part of the levee system. So here is a view of my youth home as refurbished, in 2009 and today.

Youth home-2009

With retirement I also found time to discover that my WWII service unit, 12th Armored Division had morphed into a reunion association. I joined and soon could travel with a small group of vets, wives, and some children to retrace the path through France and Germany. There were tales told and I proceeded to tell my story about our dash to secure a bridge over the Rhine River and the loss of our tank. One vet on the bus spoke thus, "Jim, I have a picture; I am standing on that tank just above that repaired final drive housing. When back home I will send you a copy." His name was Calvin Wyss and he was good to his word. I had wished to show it here, but time and my carelessness has claimed it. What I will show is a photo of citizens we visited with and the building wherein we had been held.

Heindrick Schuck &
Kathravina Albus,
Lohnsfeld, Germany

Where we spent the night
Building Became Bank after War

Wesley has been a Great Church, and still is in my book. It is the people and their hearts that make it so. Sometimes it is a sad look back at times such as the 1960's when we did evangelism by knocking on doors and sitting in living-rooms. (That was back in Edwardsville, IL.) Also sad is the loss of heritage when our children leave to find their proper future. These are normal and necessary events that spice our lives.

Yes, I have had losses. My father passed much too soon in 1971 due to a ruptured aneurysm. My blessed mother carried on to December 1998. My elder sister left us in 2008 and my other sister expired in 2016. In about 2010 it became evident that my dear wife Alice was falling under the influence of Alzheimer's Disease. I think it natural to try to allow all reasonable independence, but then one day in 2012 she slipped on the stairway of our home fell and fractured a disc in her back. In August 2013, another seeming small tumble just out of the door of our hotel room in Atlanta for my military reunion. However, it soon became evident the fall was more serious with a fractured pelvis causing internal bleeding, Thus surgery and considerable convalescence was required. Also, those frequent visits in rehab facilities took a toll on me when I contracted a very infectious intestinal bug. Shortly back home in Decatur, we were convinced by our children it was time to down-size from our home of 37 years to a single-level town house. We did celebrate our 66th anniversary in June of 2015. However, in August 2015 just two days short of her 85th Birthday and a big celebration planned, she greeted me that morning with "I am just so tired I think I will quit." I praised her for all she has done and all that has been. Then leaving her with daughter Deb, I walked to the kitchen for breakfast. Shortly with tears on her face Deb had to tell me Alice took one deep breath and just quit life on this Earth. This was such a tough moment, but I was supported with such love by the many family members who had gathered to celebrate her life and my 90 years. We did with family and wonderful Wesley family celebrate Alice's life.

Alice @ our 60th Anniversary

About to close my writing, a recent visit with my doctor caused the recall of one almost forgotten but significant event. In fall 1989 about to retire for the night, I reached for my hair brush, lifted both arms to brush my hair. A sharp pain struck as though I had been stabbed in the back. I stumbled to the bed and fell in. I lay quietly for some time. Then with an urgent need I struggled back to bathroom. Turning back toward bed I fell on my face. Alice called 911, medics carried me to Decatur General. Next, I was being tended by a young oriental doctor.

I said, "Doctor what happened."

He replied, "You bled internally. We still don't know where from, but you are unusual—you may live. Most do not. You stopped the bleeding on your own."

Well maybe not "on my own"!

Closing My Story, So Far

We know not what tomorrow brings, but as I believe we celebrate each day God allows us to live with our choices on this Planet which he created and does control.

As I close this "dissertation" you are free to question why I write. Some many may feel I am just one of very many very lucky soldiers who returned from WWII. I think there is more; at a prominent point of my life I asked God to take charge. Evidence began to build that he had accepted that invitation. Then in mid-March 1945 he told me to move, I did so, and lived. Two days later without demands of me, he tweaked the events of the day and I again escaped harm. The graces have continued. Others may assume I write for praise or glory. No, I write with a simple hope that He may be glorified. Perhaps even one reader may conclude, that with honest dedication of one's life to God's trust, they too may find events tweaked for their good.

About the Author

J AMES MARTIN FEEZEL WAS BORN in Wood River, Illinois, and served with the US Army's Twelfth Armored Division during World War II. He was stationed across both France and Germany, and he would later return home and graduate from the University of Illinois with a degree in engineering. After working for Diamond Chain in Indianapolis, Indiana, James went on to work for over thirty years with Amoco Chemical Corp. He and his wife, Alice, were married for sixty-six years before her passing, and today James lives in Decatur, Alabama.

Printed in the United States
By Bookmasters